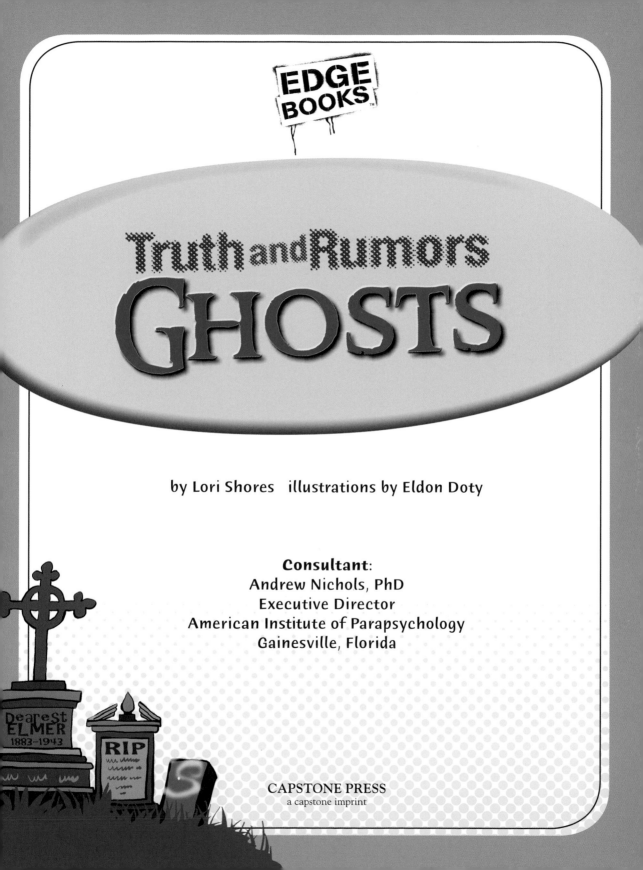

EDGE BOOKS™

Truth and Rumors
GHOSTS

by Lori Shores   illustrations by Eldon Doty

Consultant:
Andrew Nichols, PhD
Executive Director
American Institute of Parapsychology
Gainesville, Florida

CAPSTONE PRESS
a capstone imprint

Edge Books are published by Capstone Press,
151 Good Counsel Drive, P.O. Box 669, Mankato, Minnesota 56002.
www.capstonepress.com

Library of Congress Cataloging-in-Publication Data
Shores, Lori.
    Ghosts: truth and rumors / by Lori Shores; Eldon Doty, illustrator.
    p. cm. (Edge Books. Truth and Rumors)
    Includes bibliographical references and index.
    Summary: "Labels common stories about ghosts as fact or fiction and teaches readers how to tell the
difference between truth and rumors" — Provided by publisher.
    ISBN 978-1-4296-3949-1 (library binding)
    1. Ghosts — Juvenile literature. I. Title.
BF1471.S46 2010
133.1 — dc22   2009028655

Editorial Credits
Abby Czeskleba, editor; Tracy Davies; designer; Wanda Winch, media researcher;
    Nathan Gassman, art director; Laura Manthe, production specialist; Eldon Doty, illustrator

Photo Credits
Alamy: Mary Evans Picture Library 8 (bottom), Steve Speller 24 (top); Corbis: Bettmann 21
(bottom); Courtesy of Charles Walker 18 (top); Courtesy of Noreen Renier 21 (top); Fortean
Picture Library: 4, 8 (top), 9 (bottom), 10 (bottom), 12 (bottom), 20 (top); Friedrich Jürgenson
Foundation/ZKM Karlsruhe collection/unknown photographer, 1970s 22 (bottom); History
San José Research library 26 (top); Image courtesy of Gallon Historical Art, Gettysburg, PA,
www.gallon.com 14 (bottom); iStockphoto: Bill Noll cover (brown texture), Nicholas Belton
17 (top); Library of Congress: 14 (top), 15 (top); Newscom: 16 (top), William Mumler 11
(bottom); Photo submitted by 1886 Crescent Hotel and Spa, crescent-hotel.com/ghosts 29;
Shutterstock: Adam Radosavljevic front, back cover (square frame), Albachiara (quill pen/inkwell,
throughout), Ali Mazraie Shadi (halftone design throughout), Brian Weed cover (farmhouse),
Cherick 12 (top), Jill Battaglia 6, Mausinda cover (ghost woman), stock09 cover (concrete
texture), VikaSuh (gavel throughout), Winchester Mystery House, San José, CA 26 (bottom),
27 (bottom)

Table of Contents

Ghosts: Fact or Fiction? 4

Do ghosts haunt old houses? 6

Do some photos show images of ghosts?...........8

Do ghosts show themselves as
        floating lights in graveyards? 12

Do ghosts of Civil War soldiers
        haunt Gettysburg, Pennsylvania?................14

Do ghosts cause the room temperature
        to drop suddenly? 16

Can EMF meters find ghosts? 18

Can some people talk to ghosts? 20

Can ghost voices be recorded? 22

Are ghosts dangerous? 24

Is the Winchester Mystery House haunted? 26

Fact or Fiction?: How to Tell the Difference.....28

Glossary 30

Read More 31

Internet Sites 31

Index 32

Ghosts: Fact or Fiction?

Something wakes you in the middle of the night. What was that noise? As you lie there wondering, your closet door opens. Creeeeeeeeaak. It's a good thing ghosts aren't real — or are they?

Ghosts are spirits of dead people, and it's hard to know if they really exist. Even if you don't believe in ghosts, you still want answers when things go bump in the night.

FACT: A 2,000-year-old Roman ghost story tells of a ghost that appeared every night. When the house owner found bones in the yard, he buried them. The ghost was never seen again.

People around the world tell ghost stories. But is there any truth to these stories? Sorting out fact from fiction isn't always easy — especially when it comes to ghost stories. Many rumors are based on something true, even if the truth has been stretched. But with a bit of research, you can usually figure out the truth behind most rumors.

Do ghosts haunt old houses?

What's the story?

Old houses make all sorts of strange noises. These sounds can be creepy, especially on a quiet night. Is it the wind, or are ghosts having fun with us?

CONSIDER THIS . . .

Old buildings make noises at night, but that doesn't mean ghosts are to blame. Mice run through the walls and bats fly in and out of the attic. Wooden floorboards creak when the temperature drops. Creaking noises may sound like footsteps. Old pipes can make loud knocking sounds in the walls and under floors.

The VERDICT

Probably not. Before you think about calling the ghost busters' hotline, check the attic and basement. Noises may come from pipes or wooden floors. But it's also possible that strange noises are the work of rowdy ghosts. Some people claim ghosts haunt places that were special to them during their lives.

They're here … I can hear them!

Instead of a ghost, it is more likely to be …

CLANG!

SCRATCH!

SQUEAK!

CREAK!

7

Do some photos show images of ghosts?

What's the story?

In 1995, a man took a picture of England's Wem Town Hall as it burned down. He didn't see anything unusual until the photo was developed. In the picture, a little girl appears to be standing in the doorway of the burning building. The Wem Town Hall photo is not the first of its kind. Ghosts have been seen in photos before.

NOT SO FAST . . .

Spirit photography became popular in the late 1800s. People took "spirit photographs" in hopes of catching a ghost's image on film.

8

Early photography was a long process. People had to sit still for a long time to have their picture taken. If a person left halfway through, a hazy, ghost-like image would appear in the picture. Many "spirit photographs" were made this way. Modern photographers also used **double exposure** to create eerie images. These photos seem to show ghosts floating in the background. Even today, some photos show mysterious, ghost-like images.

double exposure – a photography method in which two photographs are taken on the same piece of film

Orbs — EXPOSED!

Pictures of small, floating balls of light called orbs are common examples of ghost photos. Some people believe orbs prove that ghosts were present when the picture was taken. But most photographers disagree. They say orbs are caused when a camera's flash reflects off something very small. Dust, insects, and raindrops may glow when light hits them at the right angle.

Rumor Continued

Maybe. We know how early spirit photographs were made. But that doesn't mean all ghost photos are fakes. Researchers look at negatives to see if extra images were added to photos. But pictures like the Wem Town Hall photo have never been explained. These images might be natural tricks of light, but we can't be sure.

Lincoln's Ghost Photo — EXPOSED!

Several people have reported seeing the ghost of former president Abraham Lincoln in the White House. Grace Coolidge, wife of former president Calvin Coolidge, was first to see Lincoln's ghost during the 1920s. People also claimed to have seen Lincoln's ghost during Franklin D. Roosevelt's presidency (1933-1945).

In 1871, a photograph taken by William Mumler seemed to prove Lincoln's ghost was real. But the truth behind this photo has been exposed! While sightings of Lincoln's ghost are still reported today, his ghost wasn't in the picture. Mumler's photo is simply an example of double exposure.

Do ghosts show themselves as floating lights in graveyards?

What's the story?

Graveyard visitors may be startled to see columns of wispy, floating lights. People think these mysterious lights are proof that ghosts are present.

NOT SO FAST . . .

These ghostly graveyard lights are called "will-o'-the-wisps" or "corpse fire." They also appear over marshes and other muddy areas. But people report ghosts in all sorts of places, not just graveyards and marshes. If ghosts cause these lights, shouldn't these lights show up in other places too?

The VERDICT

No. It's impossible to know when or where ghosts might appear. But they're not appearing as wisps of light in graveyards. Gases cause these strange moving lights. Rotting plants and animals release methane gas into the air. Methane burns when combined with other gases in the air. When this happens, these normally invisible gases create eerie, wispy lights.

FACT: Sir Isaac Newton mentioned these ghostly lights in his 1704 book *Opticks*.

Do ghosts of Civil War soldiers haunt Gettysburg, Pennsylvania?

What's the story?

Many Gettysburg National Cemetery visitors say they've seen ghosts of soldiers. Witnesses say the ghosts seem to be stuck in time. These ghosts act as though they are still fighting invisible enemies. Other ghosts wander as if lost but don't respond when people try to help them.

CONSIDER THIS . . .

The deadliest battle of the Civil War (1861–1865) took place in Gettysburg, Pennsylvania. In July 1863, nearly 8,000 soldiers were killed in a three-day battle. Another 40,000 men were wounded or missing by the end of the battle.

Maybe. Something ghostly seems to be happening at Gettysburg. The ghosts don't seem to notice or respond to people. Instead, the ghosts seem to be repeating terrible events from the battle. This type of sighting is known as a residual haunting. Some scientists believe battle scenes like Gettysburg leave impressions on surroundings and create these ghostly "movies."

FACT: Visitors to Gettysburg National Cemetery can take tours that describe famous ghost sightings and mysterious events.

CeMetery HiLL

Do ghosts cause the room temperature to drop suddenly?

What's the story?

Many people say ghosts create cold spots. Ghost hunters check for temperature changes to learn if ghosts are near.

WAIT A SECOND . . .

Spending time in a creepy, old house can be scary. Fear causes a person's body temperature to drop, which creates a chill. In this case, the room temperature hasn't changed. And rooms don't always heat evenly, especially in old houses. Drafts may feel like cold spots. Drafts can come from poorly insulated walls, doors, and windows. But some scientists think ghosts draw energy from their surroundings. The temperature could drop if a ghost uses heat energy in a room.

Maybe. Researchers have recorded sudden temperature changes they can't explain. But most cold spots are caused by uneven heating or drafts from open doors and windows.

FACT: Ghost hunters have recorded changes in temperature where spirits have been seen. Some temperature changes have been between six and 20 degrees.

Can EMF meters find ghosts?

What's the story?

Electromagnetic field (EMF) meters measure **electromagnetic energy**. Ghost hunters use these meters when exploring haunted houses. High energy readings are sometimes recorded in areas where ghosts were reported.

BUT CONSIDER THIS . . .

Microwaves and other machines create high amounts of electromagnetic energy. Even electrical wires give off enough energy to be picked up by an EMF meter.

Some people feel they're being watched in areas with high amounts of electromagnetic energy. Other people feel nervous or scared for no reason.

BEEP BEEP BEEP

electromagnetic energy – energy released by all matter that has a temperature greater than -460 degrees Fahrenheit (-273 degrees Celsius)

FACT: One theory about ghosts explains spirits are made up of some form of energy. If this belief is true, energy-detecting equipment could pick up a ghost's energy.

The VERDICT

Probably not. Ghost hunters use EMF meters to look for causes of ghostly activity. Sometimes ghost hunters find that high energy fields are responsible for ghost sightings and eerie feelings. But the energy from a building's bad wiring may be to blame for these feelings. Other times, there's no explanation for high energy fields. These unusual readings leave ghost hunters wondering if ghosts are to blame.

19

Can some people talk to ghosts?

What's the story?

Mediums claim they can contact ghosts. Some even say they can deliver messages between the dead and the living.

CONSIDER THIS...

People claiming they can talk to ghosts is nothing new. The ancient Greeks were some of the first people to make this claim. Even today, some people say they can speak with the dead.

Fake mediums may use a system called cold reading to fool people. Cold reading involves making guesses that are likely to be true for most people. Fake mediums do this so it seems like they know more information than they really do.

I see that you are lost and are seeking answers.

That's amazing! How did you know that?

Maybe. Remember that just because a few mediums lie doesn't mean every medium does. Some mediums, including psychic detective Noreen Renier, have helped police solve crimes.

Noreen Renier

FACT: Noreen Renier has helped police with more than 500 cases.

The Fox Sisters — EXPOSED!

In 1848, sisters Maggie and Kate Fox claimed to have an amazing talent. They said they could speak to ghosts. Ann Leah, the oldest sister, attracted crowds of people to watch her sisters. Maggie and Kate communicated with ghosts through knocking noises. Years later, the two sisters admitted they had lied. They made the noises by cracking their toes.

Maggie, Kate, and Ann Leah Fox (left to right)

Can ghost voices be recorded?

What's the story?

Friedel, can you hear me? It's mammy.

In 1959, Friedrich Jurgenson used a tape recorder to record bird songs while walking. But when he listened to the recording later, he heard voices mixed in with the birds. One voice said, "Friedel, can you hear me? It's mammy." According to Jurgenson, "Friedel" was his childhood nickname. He claimed he heard his dead mother's voice.

THE EVIDENCE

Friedrich Jurgenson

Since Jurgenson's experience, scientists and ghost hunters have used tape recorders to try to capture voices of ghosts. Thousands of recordings seem to support Jurgenson's claim that ghosts can speak through audio recorders. These recordings are known as Electronic Voice Phenomena (EVP). In most cases, no sounds are heard during the recording. But voices are heard when the tape is played back.

EVP recordings can be difficult to hear. Some people think ghosts use **white noise** to talk. Often the words are muffled and hard to understand. Sometimes the "voices" don't sound like voices at all. But even when the voices are clear, many people still aren't convinced. They say anyone could make an EVP recording by whispering into the microphone. Other people also think the recorder could be picking up radio signals.

Whooooooo! This is the voice of dead Uncle Walter.

white noise — background noise from appliances such as air conditioners and fans

Maybe. There's no real proof that a ghost's voice has ever been recorded. But that doesn't mean recording ghost voices is impossible. How do people explain the voices Jurgenson heard? Perhaps his mind was playing tricks on him. Maybe he listened to the recording so many times that he thought he heard the voice. Today, people still claim to hear ghostly voices in recordings. But it's also pretty easy to make a fake recording.

23

Are ghosts dangerous?

What's the story?

Many people believe that poltergeists are dangerous ghosts. These ghosts throw objects and start fires. So much for Casper the friendly ghost!

NOT SO FAST . . .

Scientists say ghosts have nothing to do with knives and other objects moving on their own. Studies have shown that **psychokinesis** causes this type of poltergeist activity. The activity usually happens around children or teenagers with extreme emotions. Without meaning to do anything, they use energy to move objects when they're upset.

I really hate when those guys make fun of me!

The VERDICT

Probably not. If ghosts are real, they rarely cause any harm to people. On the other hand, poltergeist activity can be dangerous. For example, fires have started without any known cause. But few scientists believe ghosts cause these mysterious events.

psychokinesis – the ability to move objects with the mind

FACT: Poltergeist means "noisy ghost" in German.

BONK!

WHACK!

25

Is the Winchester Mystery House haunted?

What's the story?

Sarah Winchester's husband died in 1881. His death left her with a great family fortune from the sale of Winchester rifles. Sarah thought that ghosts of people killed by the rifles caused her husband's death. She also believed the ghosts were haunting her. Sarah built a mansion for them so they would leave her alone. She claimed to get building instructions from the ghosts during **séances**.

THE EVIDENCE

The Winchester Mystery House is a wacky and confusing place. The house has staircases that lead nowhere and doors that open to brick walls. The house was meant to please some ghosts and trap others. Sarah believed the trick staircases and doors would confuse the bad ghosts who wanted to harm her. But rumors suggest that she was mentally ill.

The VERDICT

Maybe. Since Sarah's death in 1922, the Winchester Mystery House has been a favorite location for ghost hunters. Investigators have reported misty figures and moving lights. These events can't be explained. Mansion employees believe Sarah and ghosts of a few workers still haunt the house.

FACT: The Winchester Mystery House has 40 staircases.

séance – a meeting in which people try to communicate with spirits of the dead

FACT OR FICTION?:
How to Tell the Difference

How can you tell the difference between truth and rumors? To learn the truth, you need to figure out the facts. Try to figure out if these stories are true or false:

1. **The Crescent Hotel in Arkansas is haunted by former guests.**

2. **The cruise ship the *Queen Mary* is haunted by the ghost of a little girl.**

3. **A 2009 video from the TV show *Larry King Live* shows pop star Michael Jackson's ghost.**

Answers:
1. Maybe. The Crescent Hotel is said to be one of the most haunted hotels in the United States. Hotel guests have taken pictures of ghostly figures and orbs. The Atlantic Paranormal Society even filmed a video of a ghost. But also remember that the hotel gains attention from the reported ghost sightings.
2. Maybe. There was a little girl who drowned in the ship's pool. But that doesn't mean her ghost haunts the ship.
3. False. A closer look at the video reveals a shadow, not a ghost.

When it comes to ghosts, no one really knows the whole truth. But we know that ghostly events do happen. People hear and see things they can't explain. It's your job to ask the questions and do the research. Then you can decide the truth for yourself.

An illustration of the ghosts that are said to haunt the Crescent Hotel in Arkansas.

Glossary

double exposure (DUH-buhl ek-SPOH-zhur) — a photography method in which two photographs are taken on the same piece of film

eerie (IHR-ee) — strange and frightening

electromagnetic energy (i-lek-troh-mag-NET-ik EN-uhr-jee) — energy released by all matter that has a temperature greater than -460 degrees Fahrenheit (-273 degrees Celsius)

medium (MEE-dee-um) — a person who claims to make contact with ghosts

orb (ORB) — a small, hovering ball of light in a photograph

poltergeist (POLE-tuhr-gyst) — ghost-like activity that includes banging noises and objects moving on their own

psychic (SYE-kik) — a person who claims to sense, see, or hear things that others do not; some psychics say they can sense and communicate with ghosts.

psychokinesis (SYE-ko-kuh-nee-sis) — the ability to move objects with the mind

séance (SEY-ahns) — a meeting in which people try to communicate with spirits of the dead

white noise (WITE NOIZ) — background noise from appliances such as air conditioners and fans

Read More

Belanger, Jeff. *Who's Haunting the White House?: The President's Mansion and the Ghosts Who Live There*. New York: Sterling, 2008.

Oxlade, Chris. *The Mystery of Haunted Houses*. Can Science Solve? Chicago: Heinemann Library, 2006.

Parvis, Sarah. *Haunted Hotels*. Scary Places. New York: Bearport, 2008.

Internet Sites

FactHound offers a safe, fun way to find Internet sites related to this book. All of the sites on FactHound have been researched by our staff.

Here's all you do:

Visit *www.facthound.com*

FactHound will fetch the best sites for you!

Index

Civil War. *See* Gettysburg
cold readings, 20–21
cold spots, 16–17
Coolidge, Grace, 11
corpse fire. *See* graveyards
Crescent Hotel, 28

double exposure, 9, 11

electromagnetic energy fields
    (EMFs), 18–19
Electronic Voice Phenomena
    (EVP), 22–23

Fox sisters, 21

Gettysburg, 14–15
ghost hunters, 16, 17, 18–19,
    22, 27
ghost stories, 4, 5
graveyards, 12–13

Jurgenson, Friedrich, 22–23

Lincoln, Abraham, 11

mediums, 20–21
Mumler, William, 11

Newton, Isaac, 13
noises, 6, 7

orbs, 9

poltergeists, 24–25
psychokinesis, 24

Queen Mary, 28

Renier, Noreen, 21
residual hauntings, 15
Roosevelt, Franklin D., 11

séances, 26
spirit photography, 8–11

Wem Town Hall, 8, 10
white noise, 23
will-o'-the-wisps. *See*
    graveyards
Winchester, Sarah, 26–27